(Almost)
Everything You Need to Know
About Early Childhood Education

(Almost) Everything You Need to Know

About Early Childhood Education

**A Book
of Lists for
Teachers and
Parents**

by Judy Fujawa

gryphon house, inc. **Beltsville, Maryland**

Dedication

The thoughts, feelings and judgments in these lists come from my heart and my soul, from my mind and my spirit, and from my precious memories of an incredible journey in early childhood classrooms. Because I have had the opportunity to spend time with young children, my cup runneth over with ideas, stories, songs and memorable experiences. Those children have touched my life and left an indelible impression on my heart (and clothes).

To those children in California, Ohio, New Hampshire and Kansas, I dedicate this book of lists.

Copyright © 1998 by Judy Fujawa

Published by Gryphon House, Inc.

10726 Tucker Street

Beltsville, MD 20705

World Wide Web: http://www.ghbooks.com

Library of Congress Cataloging-in-Publication Data
Fujawa, Judy, 1941–
    (Almost) everything youneed to know about early childhood education : the book of lists for teachers and parents / by Judy Fujawa.
        p.   cm.
    Includes Index.
    ISBN 0-87659-192-6
    1. Early childhood education—Handbooks, manuals, etc. 2. Earlly childhood—Parent participation—Handbooks, manuals, etc. 3. Classroom management—Handbooks, manuals, etc. I. Title. LB
1139.23.F85   1998
372.21—dc21   98-13681
                                                  CIP

Introduction

I'm a list person. I make lists, refer to lists, recommend list-making to my friends and family, and find great pleasure and satisfaction when I can cross things off my list—like this book!

The book is written with both teachers and parents in mind, because they both work with young children and because the home-school connection is so very important. By reading these lists, parents can begin to understand and appreciate how teachers provide children with a positive early school experience, and both parents and teachers will learn ways to work together with the children in their care.

These lists have been compiled from my personal experiences in the early childhood classroom, from experiences shared by those whom I respect and from credible resources. But they are not all-inclusive, so I have left room for all of you to add to the lists, making them your own, drawing from your own personal experiences with children. These are living, changing, improving lists. Add to them, talk about them, use them when you work with children, share them with friends. This book is just the beginning!

In fact, I invite you to share the additions to the lists with me. I would welcome any new lists that you create, keeping in mind what is developmentally appropriate for young children and professionally appropriate for teachers and parents. Write to me at Gryphon House®, Inc., 10726 Tucker Street, Beltsville, MD 20705.

Acknowledgments

My husband, Tom. I call him Sunshine. He's been there for 35+ years. He is my rock, my computer wizard. "Who loves you, baby?"
My children, Gail, Greg and Scott. They nudged me along and offered long-distance support from Ohio, Georgia and California.
My family who read parts of my "work in progress" and said, "Go, girl!"

My mentor, Gale Hall, whose words and deeds nurtured me and then challenged me to grow, grow, grow! Everyone needs a "Gale" in their life.

My hero, Mimi Brodsky Chenfeld, whom I admire and try to emulate. I will always be grateful for her enthusiastic and gracious response to my book idea.

The entire staff at Title I in Nashua, New Hampshire—Pat, Sue, Brooks, June, Mary, Cindy, Brenda, Vicki, Cheryl and Lorraine. That ole' gang of mine in Windham, New Hampshire—Jeanne, Rita, Holly, Donna and Patti.

My coast-to-coast friends who epitomize the phrase, a friend in need is a friend indeed. Marianne in New Hampshire, Karol in Ohio, Gerri in Indiana and Pam in California.

My grandchildren, Brittany and Zachary, and my friend's granddaughter, Lindsay. They deserve a big "Ta-Da" for their artistic contributions.

My editor, Kathy, who has been supportive and oh, so patient. She gently guided me along as I discovered the Wonderful World of Publishing.

How to Use This Book

How about using it as a decorative paperweight!

Read an idea-a-day and refer to it like a calendar or a daily reflection.

Approach the book with a highlighter pen and mark-as-you-go, identifying those points that you want to remember.

Read the book as a resource, and use it to "jump-start" ideas that have been hibernating in the recesses of your mind.

As you read the book, expand the lists in the space provided, personalize them and make them your own.

Use it as an incentive or a challenge for your own personal growth and development.

Keep the book handy as you gather for staff and parent meetings and use it to promote discussion, to share ideas, to expand the lists, to create new lists, etc.

Sit down with a pen in hand and jot down ideas on the blank pages at the end of the book.

Keep the book in the teacher's lounge and thumb through it when you have a few minutes.

Place the book in the bathroom and consider it the "First Bathroom Book for Teachers."

Read the lists for pleasure. Enjoy them!

Table Of Contents

Teachers and Teaching (Roles, Goals and Mottos)

Teaching Is

A challenge—face it!

A responsibility—assume it!

A privilege—honor it!

Fun—enjoy it!

Rewarding—embrace it!

A lesson—learn it!

A commitment—meet it!

A performance—go for an "Oscar"!

A song—sing it!

A production—Lights! Camera! Action!

*Teaching is life—
model it!*

your additions

_____

_____

_____

_____

_____

Senses for Teachers to Nourish*

* Beyond the five senses of touch, sight, smell, taste and hearing

Sense of humor

Sense of direction

Sense of right and wrong

Sense of accomplishment

Sense of pride

Sense of inner peace

Sense of physical well-being

Sense of creativity

Sense of positive self-image

Sense of wonder

We need to nurture and model Common Sense!

your additions

_____

_____

_____

_____

_____

"Instead of" Statements

Instead of recycling old lesson plans year after year—try new ideas that work for the children you teach now!

Instead of making an example of the negative—highlight the positive

Instead of competitive games—play cooperative games

Instead of rote memorization drills—choose meaningful learning experiences

Instead of complaining about what's wrong—do something to make it right

Instead of providing a model at the art center for children to copy—encourage creative art

Instead of a teacher-directed atmosphere—provide a child-centered environment

Instead of telling a parent about problems—share successes

Instead of saying "I'm too busy"—make time

Instead of children competing against each other—strive for each child to achieve his or her personal best

Instead of sending children for a "time out"—redirect them to an acceptable activity

your additions

_____

_____

_____

_____

_____

Teachers Need

Children who love you, hug you and rub against your clothes with paint on their hands

A classroom that reflects you and your children (That "pride" thing!)

A director who supports you

Co-teachers who "complement" you (and maybe compliment you now and then)

A staff that "rallies 'round" you

Mentors who believe in you

Children's parents who respect you

Family and friends who understand you and "that thing you do"

Staff development workshops and conferences that "energize" you

A reliable vehicle big enough to transport your "stuff"

your additions

Better compensation for the endless time, energy and talent you give to your profession!

_____

_____

_____

_____

_____

How to Encourage Creativity

Provide a comfortable atmosphere where children can discover, experiment and explore.

Encourage children to ask questions and take risks.

Provide an endless supply of "stuff" for children to use to create something new.

Focus on the "process" not the product.

Provide freedom for children to create (away from your constant supervision).

Allow children to choose and use things in their own way.

Follow children's lead (don't direct them in "how to").

Allow messes.

Do something just for the fun of it (non-competitive).

Enjoy their creativity (don't force, nudge or judge).

Help children see different possibilities. ("How else could you make a bridge with the blocks?")

Your class motto:
Show me your idea!

your additions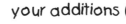

_____

_____

_____

_____

_____

Sounds You Want to Hear in Your Classroom

The sounds of children at play, better known as "joyful noise."

"Ah Ha!" sounds of discovery, surprise and success

Laughter (from children and teachers)

Conversations (two-way communication in large and small groups)

Cooperative efforts (problem-solving, taking turns)

Sounds of active learning (open-ended questions being asked, challenges being offered, etc. "How are these bottle caps the same? How are they different?")

Story-telling (stories being read, dictated, dramatized, etc.)

All types of music for singing, for dancing, for listening, etc.

Respectful words (Thank You, Please, Excuse Me)

Encouraging words (You did it!, Wow! Go for it!)

Silly sounds (rhymes, riddles, Peek-a-boo)

your additions

_____

_____

_____

_____

_____

Are the noisy and quiet activities separated?

Are the learning centers clearly defined?

Are the materials easily accessible to the children?

Do I have a non-obstructed view of all areas?

Do I have a good traffic pattern?

Have I "labeled" everything clearly?

Have I broken up the open space effectively?

Have I planned around the electric, water and light sources?

Are the messy activities on the tile and the other activities on the carpeted area?

Does the furniture and space allow for flexibility and multi-purpose uses?

Is the entire room hazard-free and safe for children?

your additions

_____

_____

_____

_____

_____

Thoughtful planning of room arrangement, equipment and supplies can eliminate many discipline problems.

"Rate Yourself" Questions for Teachers

Am I respectful of young children? (Do I ask for and value their ideas and opinions?)

Do I have a positive attitude and do I use encouraging words?

Am I child-like (wonder-filled) not childish?

Do I value "process over product"?

Do I admit my mistakes and show my human side?

Do I value creativity? Encourage creativity? Plan for creativity?

Do I enjoy children? Do I enjoy being a teacher?

Do I state what I want children to do in a positive way, rather than repeating "Don't do this" or "Don't do that"?

Do I provide a warm, encouraging and supportive environment while setting realistic limits, goals and expectations?

Do I plan for challenges, growth and success?

Rate yourself on a regular basis and strive to "be the best that you can be."

your additions

_____

_____

_____

_____

_____

New Year's Resolutions for Teachers

Lighten-up!

Talk with children, not at them.

Foster creativity!

Utilize wisely the time spent with children—interact, laugh and play.

Let go—and let them do _____. (Give up some of your control and let the children plan, execute and even evaluate projects.)

Share! Share! Share!—ideas, resources and revelations with parents, children and other teachers.

Send thank you notes directly to children's homes, addressed to the children.

Invite the children into your own home. How about a field trip to your house?

Add to your teaching portfolio on a regular basis.

Be yourself! Get Real!

Try one new idea, sing one new song, play one new game, or read one new children's book every week.

your additions

_____

_____

_____

_____

_____

Thou shall be the best role model possible.

Thou shall know when a child needs a hug.

Thou shall be able to make every child feel special.

Thou shall keep thy promises.

Thou shall be able to laugh at jokes and tell funny jokes as well.

Thou shall be able to drive a van or bus while 12 children are singing, "The Wheels on the Bus."

Thou shall know songs and stories "by heart."

Thou shall smile a lot.

Thou shall be able to draw the best out of every child.

Thou shall be able to laugh at thyself.

Thou shall celebrate diversity!

Ten Commandments for Teachers

your additions

_____

_____

_____

_____

_____

*Thou shall be a "hero"
in the eyes of every
child.*

How to Pamper Yourself to Shake, Shake, Shake That Stress Away

Treat yourself to something special—like a hot fudge sundae or a manicure.

Give yourself a "time-out" —chat with a friend over lunch or catch a movie.

Do something playful—like toss a Frisbee or jump rope.

Listen to soothing music with your feet propped up.

Relax in a fragrant bath.

Light candles and relax in a pleasant environment.

Think—the sun will come out tomorrow!

Buy fresh flowers and enjoy their beauty.

Close your eyes and let go of tension through deep breaths.

Sip hot tea or hot chocolate with marshmallows.

Don't let little things get to you—like traffic tie-ups or grocery lines (sing in traffic and think about all the good things in your life in line).

your additions

_____

_____

_____

_____

_____

Healthy Habits for Happy Teachers

Laugh a lot!

Get a good night's sleep.

Set your alarm 15 minutes early (allow time to hit the snooze button).

Wake up and start the day with a smile and a positive outlook.

Eat a good breakfast.

Take vitamins.

Drink water throughout the day.

Dress in bright, energetic colors.

Do physical and fun activities—dance, skip, etc.

Eat healthy snacks.

"Hang out" with positive-thinking people.

your additions

_____

_____

_____

_____

_____

Mottos to Practice

Acknowledge children's presence.

Honor children's requests.

Validate children's answers.

Highlight children's uniqueness.

Marvel at children's creativity.

Accommodate children's attention spans.

Protect children's innocence.

Encourage children's risk-taking.

Bolster children's self-image.

Explore children's interests.

your additions

_____

_____

_____

_____

_____

Give children the "Red Carpet" treatment AOAP (as often as possible).

Don't refer to children as kids (kids are goats).

Don't set up a teacher-focused, teacher-directed, teacher-orchestrated classroom—think child-centered.

Don't draw or use a red pencil or pen on a child's paper—ask permission before you write on a child's paper.

Don't lose respect for children—always respect them and their work!

Don't insist on a quiet classroom when children are playing (shhhhh!)—aim for a productive, happy "buzz."

Don't rely on patterns or models (copy-cat art experiences)—let the children create.

Don't recycle the same lesson plan year after year—individualize, individualize, individualize.

Don't try to be the perfect teacher who will not admit it when she makes a mistake—make them and learn from them!

Don't lose your sense of humor; laugh and encourage joyful noise—live and learn together!

Teacher Don'ts

Don't pass up spontaneous, teachable moments.

your additions

What to Include in Your Teaching Portfolio

Your resume

Letters of recommendation

An outline of your educational philosophies and your teaching goals

Evaluations from supervisors

Lesson plans

A list of resources, reference materials and inspirational reading

Short pertinent stories about your teaching experiences

Artifacts from your career (achievements, awards, acknowledgments, etc.)

Snapshots of children, your classroom and any memorable experiences

A video of you in action

Collect snapshots, samples and examples of classroom creations regularly. Date them and keep them in chronological order.

your additions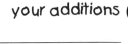

_____

_____

_____

_____

_____

Inclusions in Your Year-at-a-Glance Video

Each child

Active learning in each center

Field trips

Celebrations

Songs

Interactive large group time

Story time

Games being played (indoors and outdoors)

Creative activities (art displays, building block construction, dramatization, music and movement, etc.)

Classroom visitors sharing their gifts of time and talent

your additions

_____

_____

_____

_____

_____

Include the children in the process of producing, directing and staging the video.

How to Spot a Dedicated Teacher

He follows up on children, especially the ones he's concerned about.

She keeps up-to-date professionally by reading, participating in workshops and attending conferences.

He can be found diligently preparing for Parent-Teacher Conferences.

She goes into the classroom on weekends to set-up, put-up and make-up activities for Monday morning.

He makes new games, plans new centers and learns new songs regularly.

She goes scavenger hunting at flea markets and garage sales for things for the classroom.

He goes into the classroom prepared; he doesn't just "wing it."

She remembers to highlight each child's birthday or un-birthday.

His car (and trunk) are full of wonderful "stuff" that he collects for use in the classroom.

your additions

A dedicated teacher plans ways to make each child's early school experience a positive one.

_____

_____

_____

_____

_____

Early childhood professional books/
publications/journals/articles

Parent-child publications/magazines

Early childhood conferences/
seminars/workshops

Children's publications/magazines

Self-help books and tapes

Inspirational books/articles/tapes/videos

Spiritual books/articles/tapes/videos

Humorous books/articles/tapes/videos

Musical tapes and videos

NAEYC, Zero to Three, ACEI
Publications/Books/Pamphlets

**Teacher
Resources to
Draw on to
Keep Us
Tuned-up,
Tuned-in and
Turned-on**

your additions

_The total teacher
grows not only
professionally, but
spiritually. Keeping
your sense of humor
alive and well is
important too._

_____

_____

_____

_____

_____

During Parent/ Teacher Conferences

Share positive comments (always start with positive comments).

Share your observations (child's actions, reactions and interactions).

Show a portfolio of the child's work (drawings, stories, snapshots, etc.).

Include your concerns.

Relay personal stories about the child.

Ask for parent's input (ask questions).

Propose a cooperative effort (say, "Let's work together" and ask, "What can we do?").

Allow parents ample time to talk but stay on schedule (be considerate of the parents who are next).

Provide suggestions, recommendations or referrals at the conclusion.

Schedule a follow-up conference if necessary.

your additions

_____

_____

_____

_____

_____

Do your "home-work"...go into the conference prepared.

How to Strengthen Staff

It's important to bond socially as well as professionally, and to think TEAM.

Celebrate together.

Compliment each other.

Share ideas, songs, books, etc.

Plan regular pot-luck gatherings.

Share responsibilities like making coffee and cleaning up the staff lounge.

Attend conferences, workshops and conventions together.

Bring in homemade snacks to share. Surprise!

Acknowledge birthdays.

Leave little notes in each other's cubbies.

Keep everyone informed (post meeting notices and other important "stuff").

your additions

_____

_____

_____

_____

_____

How Children Learn

By doing (experimenting, exploring, building, planting, etc.)

Through play

Through their senses

By imitation

By making mistakes (trial and error, pain and pleasure)

By communicating

By repetition

By interacting in a supportive environment

When they are ready

When their basic needs are met

your additions

_____

_____

_____

_____

_____

Each child is wired differently. Teachers must set up their classroom to accommodate individual learning styles.

"Things" Teachers Must Provide for Active Learning to Take Place

Opportunities for observation, exploration and discovery with questions that help children look for many solutions to problems, such as, "What might happen if...?"

A variety of rich experiences

Learn-by-doing (hands-on) activities

A variety of learning materials

Wise guidance and direction as well as freedom

Books! Books! Books!

Endless supply of "stuff" for children to use in their own way

Outlets for children's ideas

Success-oriented activities

A supportive learning environment

Clearly defined and well-organized learning centers

your additions

_____

_____

_____

_____

_____

Children need to wiggle, shake, agitate! Allow it! Plan for it! Do it together! Enjoy it!

How Teachers Help Children Grow and Learn

Acknowledge their uniqueness!

Communicate with them, discuss problems together.

Emphasize the good things children do.

Set achievable goals.

Give them responsibilities.

Use positive, encouraging words.

Show them you care in what you say and do.

Respect their ideas.

Share favorite activities.

Use mistakes as opportunities to learn.

Set up situations in which they can succeed. "Tell me all you can remember about the story we just read."

your additions

_____

_____

_____

_____

_____

Emotional maturity—Is the child independent, self-motivated, able to make choices, happily involved in the classroom, etc.?

Social skills—Is the child able to get along with others, make friends, take part in conversations, etc.?

Listening skills—Is the child able to listen to stories, follow directions, focus on activities, etc.?

Oral/expressive language skills—Is the child able to express his wants and needs, repeat rhymes, songs and stories, contribute ideas, etc.?

Self-help skills—Is the child responsible for her personal belongings and her personal needs, does she clean up after herself, dress herself, etc.?

Learning skills—Is the child able to find solutions to problems, solve age-appropriate puzzles, repeat age-appropriate sequences and patterns, etc.?

Creative thinking skills—Is the child able to think divergently (see more than one solution), share new ideas, be inventive in his thinking process, etc.?

Physical skills—Is the child able to play action games, do simple exercises, participate in small and large motor activities, etc.?

Creative music and movement experiences—Is the child able to think of new ways to move, sing new words to songs, design and implement new ideas, etc.?

Positive self-esteem—Is the child growing more confident in what she can do, developing friendships, feeling good about herself, etc.?

What Children Really Need to Learn in Preschool... More Than the ABC's and the 123's

These are the things children need to learn to prepare them for kindergarten and help them develop an "I can do it!" attitude.

your additions

_____

_____

_____

Block center—You have to build the base of your block tower wider than the top.

Library center—You don't have to know how to read to enjoy a book.

Dramatic play center —It's more fun playing school when you're the teacher.

Math/manipulatives center—Math is fun when you're estimating and sorting coins.

Art center—If the bird you're drawing looks more like a dog, then why not make it a dog.

Music time—A day without music is like a day without sunshine.

Snack time—Celery with peanut butter and raisins tastes better when you call them "ants on a log."

Outdoor/playground—The harder you throw a ball at the ground, the higher it bounces.

Science center—Don't squeeze the gerbil.

Creative movement—It's more fun to make up your own actions than to just follow the directions.

Playing is more fun if you can get dirty.

your additions

_____

_____

_____

_____

_____

"Times" to Build Into Your Curriculum Every Day

Alone-time: A good time to relax and reflect

Pretending-time

Discovery-time

Creative expression-time

Socializing-time

Story-time (story-writing, story-telling, story dramatizing, etc.)

Music-time (sing, make music, listen to music, etc.)

Quiet-time (down-time)

Show me your idea!-time

Play-time indoors and outside (free choice-time)

Agitation-time (all kinds of movement, indoors and outdoors)

your additions

_____

_____

_____

_____

_____

What to Suggest When You Invite Friends, Family and Folks Into Your Classroom

Play a musical instrument.

Do magic tricks.

Share your hobby (crafts, carpentry, etc.).

Display your collectibles (shells, dolls, etc.).

Read a book or tell a story.

If you speak another language teach the children to count to ten or sing a song.

Prepare your native dish (cooking experience).

Bake cookies, decorate cookies and then eat them all up together.

Make an audiotape of a story (in English or a different home language).

Sing songs from your childhood.

Do a talent demonstration (knit, whittle, etc.).

your additions

Never pass up an opportunity to enrich the children's lives through the sharing of time, talents and treasures of others, especially grandparents.

_____

_____

_____

_____

_____

Opportunities to Acknowledge Children

When a child accomplishes something alone

When a child does better than she/he did last time(personal best)

When a child shows courage and perseverance when tackling a challenge

When a child accomplishes a self-help task (zipping a jacket, passing the serving bowl, etc.)

When a child comforts or comes to the aid of a friend in need

When a child completes a task or project

When a child shows creativity in word or deed

When a child explores and follows through with an idea

When a child takes on new responsibilities

When a child leads by example

It is an important milestone when a child accomplishes something for his or her own satisfaction and pride and not just to please the teacher.

your additions

_____

_____

_____

_____

_____

If you're wearing flannel, corduroy, etc. (types of fabric)

If you have on something plaid, striped, etc. (types of patterns)

If you're wearing red, beige, etc. (various colors)

If you have on a turtleneck, a collar, etc. (types of necklines)

If you have high-top shoes, Velcro on your shoes, etc. (types of shoes)

If you're wearing a vest, a long-sleeved shirt, etc. (types of tops)

If you're wearing jeans, shorts, etc. (types of bottoms)

If your name begins with G, with M, etc. (letters of the alphabet)

If you have blond hair, curly hair, etc. (types of hair)

If you like carrots, tomatoes, peanut butter and jelly sandwiches, etc. (types of foods)

Fun and Fair Ways to Choose Children Who Are Pleading, "Pick Me, Pick Me!"

This is a great way for children to learn patience and observation skills!

your additions

_____

_____

_____

_____

_____

The Wonderful and Powerful World of Words

What's your idea?

Show me!

What's another way!

What else?

Let's pretend!

What if (_____)? (state a circumstance like, What if you fell in a bowl of pudding?)

How else could you...?

Move like a (_____)! (object, animal, color, shape, etc.)

Phrases That "Ignite" Children Into Action

your additions

Your attitude determines the success of activities with children.

_____

_____

_____

_____

_____

_____

Phrases That Build Self-Esteem

Good thinking!

Great idea!

I knew you could do it!

You did it yourself!

Nothing can stop you now!

Looking good!

You should be very pleased with yourself!

You tried hard!

You didn't give up!

Wow! Pat yourself on the back.

your additions

_____

_____

_____

_____

_____

We need to build on children's own personal-best successes and triumphs, instead of placing them in competition against other children.

4-Letter Words Teachers Encourage Children to Use in the Classroom

Love

Wish

Care

Kind

Play

Fair

Star

Help

Hope

Draw

Okay!

Skip is a 4-letter word that lifts your spirits when you say it and when you do it.

your additions

_____

_____

_____

_____

_____

"F" Words That Children Are Allowed to Use

Friend

Fantastic

Fantasize

Fabulous

Frolic

Fanfare

Fascinate

Favorite

Fairytale

Fun

your additions

_____

_____

_____

_____

_____

The definition of forte: a person's strong point. Find it, feed it and let it flourish in every child.

Words That Are Fun to Use

Whoosh

Skedaddle

Skinamarink-a-dink-a-do

Varoom

Smithereens

Bedazzled

Zigzag

Zippity-do-da

Preposterous

Stupendous

your additions

_____

_____

_____

_____

_____

Slang words and phrases come and go. Some don't go soon enough!

Imaginative Action Words (What Do They Mean; What Do Children Think They Mean?)

Hover

Gyrate

Slither

Pounce

Transform

Swivel

Agitate

Shrivel

Inflate/deflate

Melt/freeze

your additions

The best action words that illicit the most imaginative responses are: show me!

Respectful Words

Please

Thank you

You're welcome

Excuse me

Pardon me

I'm sorry

May I?

I apologize

Forgive me

Yes, sir/Yes, ma'am

your additions

_____

_____

_____

_____

_____

What a pleasure when children model your respectful words!

What Children Say (Children Are Teachers, Too)

Children's Answers to: What's Your Favorite Thing to Do at School?

Playing school was at the top of many lists.

Play outside

Story time

Snack

Paint at the easel

Play dress-up

Build with blocks

Dance and march

Sing songs

Play in the sand

Color, cut, paste and make things

your additions

_____

_____

_____

_____

_____

When my teacher is happy to see me and gives me a hug.

When I cook with my friends and my teacher.

When my pictures are on the wall where I can see them.

When my Mom/Dad/friend/relative comes to school to help in my class.

When I see pictures of me and my family hanging in the classroom.

When I wear the Birthday Crown and everyone claps for me.

When I see my name on the Helper Chart.

When I pass out the snack.

When I can read my name all by myself.

When my teachers asks me to show everyone what I can do.

Answers to: What Happens at School That Makes You Feel Special?

your additions

_____

_____

_____

_____

_____

Sing songs that highlight children's specialness.

Ask children:

What is your favorite color?

What is your favorite book?

What is your favorite toy?

What is your favorite food?

What is your favorite song?

What is your favorite movie?

What is your favorite place?

Who is your favorite person?

What is your favorite animal?

What is your favorite TV show?

your additions

A compiled list of answers to this survey would make a great Gift Book to present to parents.

What If... Questions to Ask Children

What if it rained marshmallows?

What if cookies grew on trees?

What if lemonade came out of your faucets?

What if snow was pink cotton candy?

What if all plates were edible pancakes?

What if the telephone cord was licorice?

What if peanut butter oozed out of toothpaste tubes?

What if seat belts were made of fruit roll-ups?

What if little pizzas came out of your VCR?

What if cereal danced in your breakfast bowl?

your additions

How about creating a book of children's What Ifs?, with drawings to embellish their ideas?

_____

_____

_____

_____

_____

My mother is like a doctor because ...

My mother is like a mechanic because ...

My mother is like a cheerleader because ...

My mother is like a movie star because ...

My mother is like a teacher because ...

My mother is like a police officer because ...

My mother is like a dentist because ...

My mother is like Curious George because ...

My mother is like the President because ...

My mother is special to me because ...

Sentences for Children to Complete That Are Guaranteed to Provide Endearing and Amusing Answers

your additions ●

_____

_____

_____

_____

_____

Substitute father, aunt, grandfather, friend, etc. for mother. Write down the responses. Put in a book to make a great gift.

Parents and Teachers Working Together (Parents Are Teachers, Too)

Goals Teachers and Parents Have for Children

To develop useful skills

To learn meaningful concepts

To strive toward independence

To expand their potential

To form cooperative habits

To strive toward intrinsic motivation

To practice negotiation skills

To develop reasoning skills

To develop compassion for others

To form wholesome attitudes

To become creative thinkers and doers

your additions

_____

_____

_____

_____

_____

Our #1 goal is to guide them toward developing an "I Can Do It" self-image.

Highlights to Include in a Monthly Newsletter or Calendar

Names of teachers and all staff members, how to reach them and when they are available

Field trips

Holidays and vacations

Special days and celebrations (First Day of Winter, Red Day, Neon Day, etc.)

Themes or focus ideas (Things on Wheels, Earth Week, etc.)

Parent and volunteer schedules (include the time, talent or treasure they will be sharing)

Reminders and requests (Picture Day, Classroom Needs List, etc.)

Thank you's and acknowledgments

Daily classroom schedule and routine

Parent education articles or words of inspiration

your additions

_____

_____

_____

_____

_____

A monthly newsletter or calendar is a valuable tool for communicating.

What are your child's favorite outdoor activities?

List five of your child's favorite around-the-house activities.

What activities do you do together with your child or as a family on evenings, weekends, holidays?

What are your child's special talents or strong points?

In what areas does your child need growth and development?

What are your child's responsibilities or chores at home?

Does your child have any physical limitations?

What are your child's favorite foods and snacks? Any dislikes?

What trips have you taken with your child recently?

What television programs does your child watch? Alone? With you?

your additions

_____

_____

_____

_____

_____

"Getting to Know You" Questions for Parents to Answer About Their Child

Each answer helps to paint a picture of the total child.

If it hurts, stop doing it!

You can write a good story, even though you can't spell or write—dictate it to your teacher.

Chocolate chip cookies taste best when they are right out of the oven.

When you get angry stamp your feet or punch a pillow.

If you forget the tune make up your own.

Poems don't have to rhyme.

Anything can be a toy.

"Last is best" isn't always true.

Your shadow will do what you do.

More isn't always better.

Oranges taste best when they are real, not when they're popsicles or soda or flavored candy.

Common Sense Lessons Children Learn Sooner or Later

Treat others the way you want to be treated. It makes sense!

your additions

_____

_____

_____

_____

_____

Simple Requests: Children Ask Their Parents to...

Be a good role model

Answer my questions

Be firm and consistent

Spend time with me

Read to me

Say "I love you" to me and to each other

Give me hugs and kisses and pats on the back and give each other hugs, kisses and pats on the back

Let me see your mistakes and help me learn from my mistakes

Don't spoil me by giving me everything I ask for

Keep yourself healthy—take care of yourself for me

Be patient with me. I'm a work in progress.

your additions

Warm and Wonderful Ways to Build Memories With Children

Sing together (makeup songs)

Listen to the rain together (or the wind, or the birds, etc.)

Fly kites together

Make mud pies together

Make dandelion crowns together

Draw pictures on the sidewalk with chalk

Have a tea party together

Take walks/ride bikes together

Play games (makeup games)

Read together

your additions

The key word is together. While you're at it, take a few snapshots to capture the moment.

_____

_____

_____

_____

_____

Games to Teach Children From Your Own Childhood

- Hopscotch
- Pick-up Sticks
- Go Fish
- Checkers
- Chinese jump rope
- Follow the Leader
- Kick-the-can
- Hide and seek
- Marbles
- Dominoes
- Jump rope (include some of your favorite rhymes and chants)

your additions

_____

_____

_____

_____

_____

*When you're outside
play games together!*

Things That Scare Little Children

Thunder and lightening

Spiders

Monsters

Things that go "bump" in the night

Shadows

Bad dreams

Witches

Being left alone/being lost

Parents who argue/fight

Parents/teachers who threaten

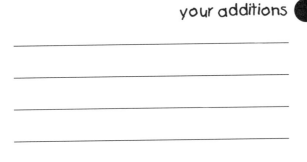

your additions

_____

_____

_____

_____

_____

The real-life traumas reported on nightly news.

When Children Could Use a Hug

When they are happy

When they are sad

When they are scared

When they are tired

When they are anxious

When they are angry

When they are frustrated

When they are lonely

When they are rejected

When they are proud

your additions

Actually, a hug is welcome at any time.

_____

_____

_____

_____

_____

Things Found in Children's Pockets

Things from nature like sticks and stones and pine cones

Collectibles like baseball cards or stickers

Formerly living things like roly-poly bugs and creepy crawlies

Things Mom puts in like tissues and mittens

Folded-up things like school newsletters and permission slips

Throw-away things like used bandages and broken shoelaces

Coins or money

Wadded-up things like candy and gum wrappers

Little toys and game pieces

Things that clog washing machines like sand or playdough

your additions

_____

_____

_____

_____

_____

Children would rather have clothes with pockets than clothes without pockets.

A plain white T-shirt, banner or tote bag along with fabric paints and markers

A special book accompanied by an audio tape of you reading the book

A dress-up suitcase full of clothes, hats, jewelry, ties, vests, boas, face paint, costumes, etc.

A creative art kit consisting of a wide variety of creative art supplies

A memory game made out of snapshots (double prints) of the child

A bucket-o-ingredients including recipes for playdough, bubble solution, face paint, etc.

A toolbox full of safe miscellaneous tools, measuring devices, a child-sized apron and a whole supply of wood pieces

A coupon book made by you with special coupons highlighting activities, privileges, fun foods, etc.

A gardening kit made up of gardening tools, various seeds, flower pots, soil and a watering can in a handy gardener's basket

A jewelry box kit consisting of a plain wooden box to decorate and a variety of decorative items like gemstones, glitter, lace, sparkles, beads, etc. (glue, too)

Creative Gift Ideas for the Children in Your Life

When in doubt about gift-giving, just remember back to what you enjoyed as a child.

your additions

_____

_____

_____

Books, Stories and Reading

Read books to your child every day for at least 20 minutes; look at the words and illustrations and discuss the story after you read it.

Re-read the books your child requests; ask your child to "read" the story to you.

Talk with your child a lot.

Tell family stories.

Check out books from the library with your child's own library card.

Buy books for you and your child, buy books as gifts for others.

Sing songs regularly.

Repeat rhymes.

Set up a cozy nook or cranny as a reading area in your home.

Keep books in the car for "waiting" times.

Include your child in meaningful correspondence (letters, postcards, Thank You notes).

Take part in purposeful reading (instructions, recipes, directions).

Keep a variety of reading materials available (newspapers, magazines, etc.).

Model the love of reading by reading for pleasure.

The best thing parents can do is to form positive attitudes about reading so that their child will want to learn to read.

your additions

_____

_____

_____

Reading provides precious time together.

Reading promotes closeness (sitting together or lying side by side).

Reading enhances intellectual skills like sequencing, classifying, predicting outcomes, etc.

Reading expands children's experiences of new people, places and things.

Reading feeds the imagination.

Reading develops listening skills.

Reading builds a positive association with the printed word, which encourages children to want to learn to read.

Reading builds language skills.

Reading is a way to access information and learn facts.

Reading fosters a respect and appreciation for books.

Answers to: Why Read to My Child?

Reading is enjoyable and encourages children to learn throughout their lives.

your additions ●

_____

_____

_____

_____

_____

The Little Engine That Could by Watty Piper

Corduroy by Don Freeman

Caps for Sale by Esphyr Slobodkina

Goodnight Moon by Margaret Wise Brown

The Little House by Virginia Lee Burton

Brown Bear, Brown Bear What Do You See? by Bill Martin Jr.

The Snowy Day by Jack Ezra Keats

Make Way for Ducklings by Robert McCloskey

Are You My Mother? by P. D. Eastman

The Very Hungry Caterpillar by Eric Carle

The Napping House by Audery Wood

I Have to Go! by Robert Munsch

The Rainbow Fish by Marcus Pfister

your additions

_____

_____

_____

_____

_____

Books Children Want Read to Them Again, and Again and Again

Reading a favorite book is like visiting a best friend.

Things to Do With a Story Book

Look at the pictures

Read it

Re-read it (children love repetition)

Review it (re-tell it, without actually reading it)

Discover the sequence

Dramatize it (act it out)

Revise it (change the title, change the characters, etc.)

Make pictures about it

Encourage children to read along

Personalize it (revise or dramatize it using children's names instead of the characters' names, or change the situation to match one happening now)

your additions

_____

_____

_____

_____

_____

If the book is also a song, sing it! Then, clap it, snap it, tip it, tap it and then do it all over again.

Props to Use With a Book or a Story

Flannelboard

Puppet

Pocket chart

Flip chart

Pictures

Records, tapes, musical instruments

Objects that relate to the story

Story apron

Costumes/masks

Laminated cutouts made from scenes and characters from books (use a copy machine)

your additions

_____

_____

_____

_____

_____

_____

Using a flashlight in a darkened room during story time is just plain fun (especially if it's a suspenseful or adventurous story)!

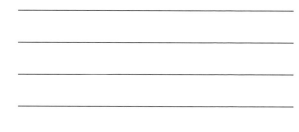

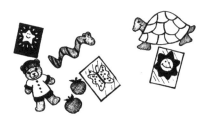

The Gingerbread Man—gingerbread

Stone Soup—vegetable soup

Blueberries for Sal—blueberry muffins

Bread and Jam for Frances—bread and jam

White Snow, Bright Snow—snowman-shaped cake

The Carrot Seed—raw carrots with dip or cooked and glazed carrots

The Thanksgiving Story—pumpkin pie

Chicken Soup With Rice—chicken soup with rice

Jamberry—jam

If You Give a Mouse a Cookie—cookies

Book and Recipe Combinations

Books and cooking experiences are an enjoyable combination; they also are a great way to learn math skills, language skills, how to work with others, how to share and lots more.

your additions

_____

_____

_____

_____

_____

Familiar Stories That Adapt to Dramatization and Puppetry

The Three Little Pigs

Goldilocks and the Three Bears

The Little Red Hen

Jack and the Beanstalk

The Gingerbread Man

The Three Billy Goats Gruff

Henny Penny

Chicken Little

Caps For Sale

Mother Goose Rhymes

When in doubt, ask the children for their ideas and then you're off to a delightful experience.

your additions

_____

_____

_____

_____

_____

Layered Books

Step by Step Books

Pop-Up Books

Slide-Out Books

Tri-Fold Books

Pocket Books

Window Books

Accordion Books

Flap Books

Story-Block Books

Types of Books That Children Like to Make

your additions

_____

_____

_____

_____

_____

*Big books are always
a big hit with children.*

Provide an area for book-making and label it.

Keep supplies available every single day.

Rotate a variety of supplies.

Print children's words exactly as they dictate them.

Create a Class Book once a month (it's a bonding experience as well as a cooperative effort).

Highlight "special" days like New Supplies Day, Shape Book Day, Book About Me Day, etc.

Acknowledge the children's completed books (read it, display it, etc.).

Label their books (title, author, illustrator).

Utilize the book-making center yourself (modeling).

Ask for and then implement the children's book-making ideas.

 Tips for Book-Making With Children

Your enthusiasm and support for the Book-Making Center will be contagious!

your additions

_____

_____

_____

_____

_____

Supplies to Keep in the Book-Making Center

Crayons, markers, pencils and other writing utensils

Paper for book pages (note paper, typing paper, computer paper, etc.)

Paper for book covers (construction paper, wallpaper, wrapping paper, etc.)

Items to hold pages together (stapler, brads, rings, yarn, etc.)

Hole punch

Scissors

Ruler

Glue and tape

Samples and examples of various types of books

Magazines, calendars, catalogs, greeting cards, etc.

Refurbish and rotate supplies on a regular basis. Add eye-catching items like stamps and stickers once in a while.

your additions

_____

_____

_____

_____

_____

Qualities of a Gifted Storyteller

Reads the story beforehand and is familiar with the story before reading it to children

Has a "gotcha" introduction to the story

Includes the children in the storytelling process

Keeps illustrations and text visible

Uses props effectively

Reads with appropriate vocal inflection

"Hams it up" with appropriate facial expressions

Edits the story when necessary to make it more appropriate for children

Allows questions and comments, yet still holds the children's interest while continuing the story

Recaps the story at the end

Plans an appropriate follow-up

Children sense when the teacher knows the story by heart; they also know when the teacher puts a lot of "heart" into story-telling.

your additions

Essentials for Learning

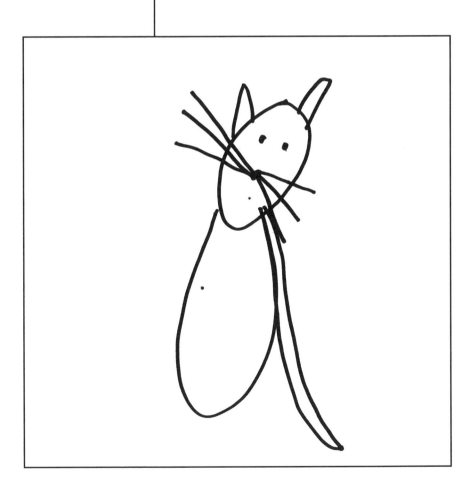

How You Know That Learning Is Taking Place

Thoughts are shared

Questions are asked

Answers are discovered

Challenges are offered

Suggestions are implemented

Structures are constructed

Books are utilized

Music and movement are explored

Ideas are "created"

Successes are celebrated

your additions

_____

_____

_____

_____

_____

While all of this active learning is taking place noise is happening!

Retell and record a "happening"

Give directions

Summarize learning

Evaluate an activity

Promote creative writing

Record ideas

Initiate a project

List criteria

Reinforce skills

Celebrate an occasion

Use an Experience Chart to

your additions ●

_____

_____

_____

_____

_____

*An experience chart is
a wonderful, visual
example of children's
words put into print.*

Basic "Props" for Teachers to Keep on Hand in the Classroom

Magic wand (could be just a stick with a star glued on the end)

Tambourine (could be homemade)

Crown (could be a decorative, ornate crown or just the Burger King variety.

Megaphone/microphone (could be just a stick with a Styrofoam ball on top)

Cheerleader pompoms (could be made with newspaper)

Puppet (could be one from your own childhood)

Decorative box, bag or scarf (for hiding mystery objects)

Parachute (could be a bed sheet cut into a circle)

Flashlight (accompanied by new batteries)

Camera (with a supply of film and new batteries)

Decorative "eye-shades" would be great to have on hand for those special "Hide Your Eyes!" guessing games.

your additions

_____

_____

_____

_____

_____

Supplies or Materials That Encourage Children to Be Creative

Paper, crayons, markers, tape, glue, etc.

Playdough

Blocks

Balls

Sand

Water

Fabric pieces

Dress-ups and prop boxes

Boxes, boxes, boxes

Lots of discarded "stuff" to make "new stuff"

● your additions

_____

_____

_____

_____

_____

*A process-oriented
format as well as
open-ended activities
allow creativity to
blossom.*

Varieties of Paper to Keep Handy

Newsprint

Butcher paper

Manila paper

Construction paper

Wallpaper

Crepe paper

Tissue paper

Adding machine paper

Wax paper

Computer paper

your additions

Donated paper (from parents, friends and stores) can provide the amount and the variety needed.

Favorite Dress-Ups in the Dramatic Play Center

Feathery boas

Dazzling necklaces and bracelets

Twirly skirts

Sparkly tops

Shiny, patent leather purses

Tasseled western boots

Fringed vests

Sequined high-heeled shoes

Brimmed hats

Silky scarves

Costumes

your additions

Children love to play Let's Pretend, so it's important to provide a variety of articles that encourage and promote fun.

Sand (or water) and pebbles, rocks, shells, etc. ●

Water (warm, cold, colored, soapy, etc.)

Sand (dry, wet, colored)

Dirt/mud

Water and sponges

A messy art project

Large marbles and sand (or water)

Various frozen ice forms

Birdseed (then scatter to feed the birds)

Gelatin molds

Goop (half cornstarch and half water mixture)

Various sand/water accessories (toys, molds, funnels, sifters, etc.)

Manipulatives to Place in the Sand/Water Table

your additions

Overstimulated or anxious children can be re-directed to the sand/water table for a calming and soothing experience. It works!

_____

_____

_____

_____

_____

_____

Animal Accessories to Rotate in and out of Centers

Jungle animals

Farm animals

Forest animals

Desert animals

Prehistoric animals

Insects

Zoo animals

Sea animals

Domestic animals

Arctic animals

Mix-and-match combo

your additions

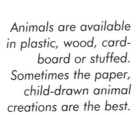

Animals are available in plastic, wood, cardboard or stuffed. Sometimes the paper, child-drawn animal creations are the best.

Things to Do With Boxes

Build, stack, sort, line-up, etc.

Encourage children to make them into a rocket, train, telephone booth, etc.

Turn upside down for additional table space.

Crawl into them and tunnel through them.

Paint and decorate them with the children.

Cut various sized holes to create a target game, peek-a-boo center, etc.

Make decorative room dividers.

Create a "be alone" space.

Use to display children's art.

Set up as a puppet theater, TV or video screen for dramatic arts experiences.

Arrange for storage, storage, storage.

How about a box decorated like a birthday cake, big enough for a child to popout of the cake.

your additions

_____

_____

_____

_____

_____

Collectibles for Counting and Sorting

Keys

Buttons, buttons, buttons (the larger the better)

Ceramic tiles

Plastic bottle caps

Discarded puzzle pieces, game pieces

Playing cards

Shells

Rocks

Bag of rubber bands of various sizes and colors

Plastic blocks or wooden blocks

Beads

your additions

_____

_____

_____

_____

_____

Carpet squares make great individual mats for defining a sorting space. Masking tape can be used to define the space on each mat.

"Wow" Things to Print With

An old shoe

Fly swatters

Toilet bowl plungers (new ones)

Bubble wrap

Various parts of the body (elbow, knee, foot, etc.)

Wads of wrinkled-up newspaper

Mesh pot scrubbers

Sponges (various sizes and shapes)

Kitchen utensils

Bingo markers

Old toys (or parts or pieces of old toys)

your additions

_____

_____

_____

_____

_____

Wanted: Discarded items with interesting and unusual surfaces.

Varieties of Brushes to Paint With

Toothbrush

Vegetable brush

Make-up brush

Toilet bowl brush (new)

Hair brush

Scrub brush

Clothes brush

Shoeshine brush

Nail brush

Sponge brush

How about a different brush each week?

your additions

_____

_____

_____

_____

_____

What Children Might Do With a Piece of Newspaper

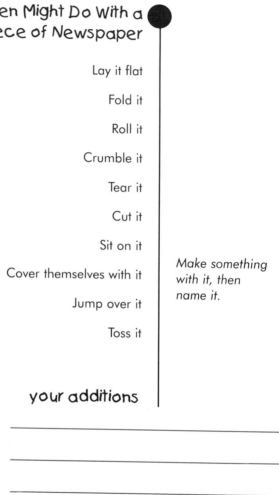

Lay it flat

Fold it

Roll it

Crumble it

Tear it

Cut it

Sit on it

Cover themselves with it

Jump over it

Toss it

Make something with it, then name it.

your additions

_____

_____

_____

_____

_____

Things to Make From a Piece of Newspaper

A paintbrush

A baton

Balls

Confetti

A telescope

A "toot-toot-tooter" horn

A hat

Rhythm sticks

Pompoms

A paper airplane

Ask the children what other ideas they have. A piece of newspaper can be used many ways.

 your additions

Weaving Supplies

- Yarn
- Fabric strips
- String
- Rope
- Pipe cleaners
- Twist ties
- Notions (lace, ribbon, elastic, rickrack, bows, etc.)
- Things from nature (sticks, vines, feathers, leaves, etc.)
- Classroom "memorabilia" (broken shoe laces, string from balloon bouquets, ribbon from birthday packages, etc.)
- Paper strips (newspaper, construction paper, wrapping paper, etc.)

Weave on a fence, sports netting or chicken wire attached to an old picture frame.

your additions

_____

_____

_____

_____

_____

Popular Props for Active Play

Parachute

Streamers

Balls

Fabric pieces

Hula hoops

6-ft. (1.8m) piece of ribbon on a stick

Elastic stretchies

Balloons (with careful supervision)

Ropes

Scarves

your additions

_____

_____

_____

_____

_____

The tambourine is a must-have. You can shake it, tap it, rattle and roll it, up and down and all around.

"Tossables" for Parachute Fun

- Balls
- Balloons
- Bells
- Rope pieces
- Stuffed animals
- Paper cutouts (hearts, cloverleafs, etc.)
- Feathers
- Newspaper wads
- Scarves
- Pairs of mittens, socks, shoes, etc.

your additions

Sometimes a bed sheet works better than a parachute because it doesn't have a hole in the middle and it can be big or little.

Items to Place in an Obstacle Course

Tires (bicycle, automobile, truck, tractor, etc.)

Ropes

Hula hoops

Balance beams/wooden planks

Tunnels

Slides

Safety cones

Barrels/boxes

Rope swing

Step ladder (lying flat)

your additions

_____

_____

_____

_____

_____

*Always keep in mind
the following slogan:
Safety first, last and
always.*

Sources for Usable Discards (Better Known as Beautiful Junk!)

Carpet stores (carpet pieces)

Printing shops (paper, paper, paper)

Appliance stores (boxes)

Shoe stores (shoe boxes)

Locksmith (keys)

Wallpaper stores (wallpaper samples)

Decorator shops (fabric)

Kitchen and bath supply stores (ceramic tiles, linoleum, etc.)

Grocery stores (paper bags, store displays, etc.)

Lumber yard, hardware store or high school wood shop (wood scraps)

Framing stores (matte board)

Sign-maker shops (sticky letters, sticky strips, etc.)

your additions

Parents (and friends, neighbors and family members) can be your best source for beautiful junk.

_____

_____

_____

_____

_____

What Children Love: Music, Moving and Singing

What to Do With Music

Listen to it

Dance to it

Clap to it

Move with it

Sing along with it

Keep a rhythm going with it

Play instruments along with it

Make up words to it

Appreciate it

Make-believe with it

your additions

How about asking the children to close their eyes and visualize soothing or calming images in their mind?

Things to Do to the Beat of a Rhythm Instrument

Breathe to the beat

Exercise to the beat

Change partners to the beat

Change body shapes to the beat

Skip, run, hop, crawl and move to the beat

Move your body to the beat

Change facial expressions to the beat

Change your voice to the beat

Sing to the beat

Keep rhythm to the beat

Paint or draw to the beat

your additions

After exploring these ideas, ask two or more children to create something together.

_____

_____

_____

_____

_____

B-I-N-G-O

Songs Children Never Tire of Singing Just One More Time

If You're Happy and You Know It

I'm a Little Teapot

Eensy Weensy Spider

Old MacDonald

The Wheels on the Bus

Where Is Thumbkin?

5 Little Speckled Frogs

There Were 10 in the Bed

Of course, Happy Birthday to You is always fun to sing (especially on your birthday).

your additions

_____

_____

_____

_____

_____

C-O-L-O-R	**5-Letter Words That Can Be Made Into a Song to the Tune of B-I-N-G-O**
S-M-I-L-E	
D-A-N-C-E	
C-O-U-N-T	
B-U-I-L-D	
S-H-A-R-E	
S-N-A-C-K	
P-A-I-N-T	
S-T-O-R-Y	
L-A-U-G-H	

your additions ●

_____

_____

_____

_____

_____

What child hasn't learned how to spell by happily singing this song!

"Zipper-In" Versions of Who Stole the Cookie?

Who Stole the Pumpkin From the Pumpkin Patch?

Who Stole the Apple From the Apple Tree?

Who Stole the Honey From the Honey Pot?

Who Stole the Snowballs From the Snowball Fort?

Who Stole the Candy From the Candy Jar?

Who Stole the Pennies From the Piggy Bank?

Who Stole the Veggies From the Garden Plot?

Who Stole the Flowers From the Flower Bed?

Who Stole the Buttons From the Button Kit?

Who Stole the Crayons From the Crayon Box?

your additions

Children love to "zipper-in" their own ideas to familiar songs, rhymes and games.

_____

_____

_____

_____

_____

Favorite, Familiar Tunes That Are Easy to Sing, Change and Rearrange

Twinkle, Twinkle, Little Star

The Farmer in the Dell

Old MacDonald

Jingle Bells

Happy Birthday

The Wheels on the Bus

B-I-N-G-O

Row, Row, Row Your Boat

If You're Happy and You Know It

Skip to My Lou

London Bridge

your additions

_____

_____

_____

_____

_____

*Include the children's
names as often as
possible when creating
a new song.*

Musical Games and Dances Children Love

Hokey Pokey

Farmer in the Dell

The Freeze

Looby Lou

Body Rock

The Bunny Hop

YMCA

Shake My Sillies Out

The Chicken Dance

The Macarena

your additions

_____

_____

_____

_____

_____

These games and dances are even more valuable and creative when children are allowed to create their own words and actions, and even make their own props to accompany the fun!

Suggestions, Tips and Other Good Stuff

Things to Do With a New Idea, Activity, Game or Song

Do it with children

Do it again (especially if it didn't work too well)

Change it to meet children's needs

Adapt it to meet your talents

Rearrange it for your classroom situation

Combine it with other classroom activities

Improvise (be creative)

Implement ideas that children suggest

Do it again! Children love repetition, repetition, repetition!

You can "THUMBPRINT" any idea...mold it and make it your own.

your additions

_____

_____

_____

_____

_____

Pie Tins, Pizzas and Merry-go-rounds

Flags, Fairies and Flying Things

Bagels, Wheels and Lifesavers

Magic, Dreams and Pretend Things

Silhouettes, Handprints and Snapshots

Rain, Teardrops and Wet Things

Bears, Beards and Hairy Things

Applause, Bows and Things to Cheer About

Razzle Dazzle, Glitter and Things That Sparkle

Jokes, Riddles and Things That Make You Giggle

New Projects/ Themes (Think About Them; Talk to Children About Them)

● your additions

_____

_____

_____

_____

_____

*Design your own
projects/themes based
on the interests, talents
and ideas of your
children.*

Beginnings: like the first signs of spring or starting a button, stamp or sticker collection

Events of the day: like a Frantic Friday or an Unbirthday Day

Milestones: like losing a tooth or a 5th birthday

Accomplishments: like recognizing their names on their cubbies or learning to tie their shoes

Diversity: like highlighting different cultures or sharing unique traditions

Family events: like a new brother or a grandmother's visit

Appreciation of nature: like a beautiful rainbow or a seed sprouting

Exciting news events: like a shuttle launch or a Mars landing

Good deeds: like a class clothing drive or a food basket collection

Endings: like completing a Book Fair or the last day of the school year

Occasions to Celebrate With Children

Emphasize the child-centered experiences that are meaningful, instead of focusing on holidays and routine calendar events.

your additions

_____

_____

_____

_____

_____

"Special" Days

Backwards day

Mixed-up, mismatched day

Mud day

Red day (or any other color)

Pajama day

Hat day

Inside-out day

Beach/Hawaii day

Book-swap day

Teddy bear share day

your additions

_____

_____

_____

_____

_____

*Plan a costume day
for any other month
except October.*

What a Hula Hoop Can Be

Steering wheel

Clock

Vacuum cleaner

Circular window

Washing machine/dryer

Swimming pool

Boat

Bubble

Merry-go-round

Wishing well

your additions

Twirling a hula hoop is difficult for young children, but imagining what else it could be is always possible.

What Else a Carpet Square Can Be

Magic carpet

Stage

Skateboard

Sled

Home plate

Umbrella

Cape

Shield

Plane/train/car

Flotation device

The more you ask children, the more creative their responses become.

your additions

_____

_____

_____

_____

_____

Classroom Activities and Ideas That Work Year After Year

Send home "Something Good Happened Today" notes on a regular basis

Decorate and set out an "I Can" can for children to fill

Put out "Material of the Month" (use recycled materials) and ask children to create a machine or invention

Do a complete body tracing on large rolls of paper and watch the fun begin as children color in their features and clothing

Gather together for a monthly sing along

Compile a child-dictated recipe book to give parents as a gift

Prepare Stone Soup as a class community, with each child contributing a vegetable to the pot

Send a monthly calendar of classroom activities, events and highlights to parents

Organize a book swap—each child brings two books to trade (only mutually agreed-upon trades are allowed)

The ideas that re-surface every year could become your trademark activities.

your additions

_____

_____

_____

_____

_____

Things Children Love to Draw

Lines, squiggles and blobs

Their selves

Family

House

Hearts

Rainbow

Sun

Flowers

Trees

Grass

"Smiley" faces

your additions

Children like to draw pictures of their teachers, too. Save as many as you can. Make a book that you will treasure.

_____

_____

_____

_____

_____

Child-Made Gifts Parents Will Treasure

A calendar with children's art

Their child's handprint in plaster or on paper

A child-decorated picture frame with their child's photo in it

A child-decorated Memory Box for collecting all those precious creations brought home

A book entitled, Children's Answers to Important Questions, with the answers dictated to the teacher

A child-decorated ornament with their child's photo on it and labeled with the year

A laminated display folder of their child's self-portrait, one drawn in September and the other at the end of the school year

Flowers grown from seeds in a child-embellished flower pot

your additions

A photo of their child on anything that has been decorated by their child will be con- sidered "a keeper."

_____

_____

_____

_____

_____

Things That "Snuff Out" Creativity

Coloring books

Ditto sheets

Competition, awards and rewards

Relying on demonstrations that show the "right way" to do something

"No mess" rules

"Shhhh" atmosphere

Teacher hovering

Models, prototypes and examples for children to copy

Asking questions that have only one right answer (What color is this? How many circles are on this page?)

Providing instant answers to children's questions, ignoring children's questions or not allowing questions

A "stifling" classroom atmosphere with restricted choices, supplies and materials

An environment that adopts a "teacher-may-I" format will suffocate creativity.

your additions ●

_____

_____

_____

_____

_____

How Children Can Release Tension

- Manipulate wet clay

- Punch a punching bag or pillow

- Hammer nails into a tree stump (while supervised)

- Dig, dig, dig in the sand

- Take a hike

- Play at the water table or in a pool of water (while supervised)

- Climb on indoor/outdoor gymnastic equipment

- Participate in vigorous movement games

- Do exercises like jumping-jacks, somersaults, etc.

- Sing and move with songs like "Shake My Sillies Out"

- Bounce on a mattress or trampoline

your additions

_____

_____

_____

_____

_____

Each child has his or her own stress-level. Sometimes just being alone will work wonders.

Older People and Young Children Enjoy the...

Power of a touch

Warmth of a hug

Reassurance of a smile

Lightheartedness of laughter

Comfort of a song

Gift of storytelling

Spirit of friendship

Luxury of time

Memory of a precious moment

Anticipation of another gathering—tomorrow!

● your additions

Each generation gives to the other the most priceless gift of all: each other!

_____

_____

_____

_____

_____

Intergenerational Activities Enjoyed by Young and Old

Reading and telling stories

Simple physical exercises set to music/song

Easy baking projects

Eating snacks/treats

Playing simple games

Puppet-making and dramatizing stories

Good ole' sing-alongs

Music-making (with or without instruments)

Un-birthday celebrations

Cuddling pets

your additions

_____

_____

_____

_____

_____

*Hand-holding and
conversation provide
"warm fuzzies" for all*

Combinations That Go Together as Naturally as the Intergenerational Blending of Young and Old

Cookies & milk

Hugs & kisses

Fresh fruit & yogurt

Peanut butter & jelly

Popcorn & movies

Hot chocolate & marshmallows

Crayons & paper

Giggles & laughter

Fall days & a walk in the park

Apple pie & ice cream

Cheese & crackers

Books & quiet time

Snow & making a snowman

your additions

"Adopt" senior citizens; the time that they spend with the children will be as rewarding for them as for the children.

_____

_____

_____

_____

_____

Non-Verbal Greetings

Wave

Wink

High-five

Thumbs-up

Throw a kiss

Smile

Hug

Shake hands

Applause

Fist-jive (One Potato, Two Potato motion)

your additions

It's important to greet your co-teachers as well as the children.

_____

_____

_____

_____

_____

_____

"Listen-Up" Signals

Countdown slowly from 10 to 1

Place your finger over your mouth in a "shhhh" fashion

Cup your hand around your ear

Hold two fingers up in the air

Make an attention-getting trumpet sound (the kind you hear at the beginning of a race)

Say "Freeze!"

Recite a child-composed rhyme or poem

Say, "Stop, Look" then spell out "L-I-S-T-E-N" slowly

Make a "time-out" signal like a referee

your additions ●

_____

_____

_____

_____

_____

Giving children warnings that a transition is about to happen is the best signal, but there are times when having a familiar "Listen-Up" signal is a helpful tool.

your list

your highlight
or wrap-up
phrase

_____

_____

_____

_____

_____

Name

Address

City

State/Zip

your list

_____

_____

_____

_____

_____

_____

_____

_____

_____

_____

Name
_____

Address
_____

City
_____

State/Zip
_____

your highlight or wrap-up phrase

Index